Reiki's Hidden Jewels

- A Transmission -

by
Mynavati

Cover Design, Craig McQueenie - craig@rockpawdesign.com

Reiki Symbol

Universal Life Force Energy

**Dedication in
honour and gratitude
of**

Mikao Usui

the Divine Vehicle

who rediscovered, expounded, followed and taught

what we now know as Reiki

Gratitude to my Reiki Lineage

and to all the Reiki Practitioners I have had the privilege

to Initiate and share Sacred Reiki Space

Table of Contents

Chapter 9

Chapter 10

Chapter 11

Coda

Epilogue

Prelude

These writings are for those interested in Reiki Initiation, for those who are already Initiated and for those seeking an understanding of Reiki on any level.

The book is not a practical handbook of Reiki that explains either its history or practice. It does not show hand placements and it does not guide you how to heal.

It does not give you drawn symbols and it does not purport to make you a Reiki healer. There are many books written about Reiki which you can access that can give you this kind of information.

This book is however an exploration and a transmission of the true meaning of Reiki energy and Reiki healing transmitted to me over many years through a series of revelations and realisations. It is a personal sharing of my awareness of Universal Wholeness.

If you are not yet initiated into Reiki, I hope that these writings encourage you to enter the fathomless Spiritual Path of Reiki and Reiki Healing through the first steps of Reiki Initiation.

If you are already Initiated, my prayer is that this view of Reiki will assist you and accompany you on your ever-increasing Journey towards the Divine wonder of Universal Wholeness.

Reiki's Hidden Jewels-A Transmission

Forward

Here, the meaning of Reiki,
Universal Life Force Energy
is synonymous
with
Universal Wholeness,
Divine Love,
God

God, is not a copyright of any religion, form, idea or
personality.
God is who and what you believe God is.
God is the Divine within you and within
everyone and everything.

Reiki is Universal Wholeness,
Universal Wholeness is God,
Reiki is God, is Universal Wholeness…
All is One
All is Divine Love

Reiki Initiation

Japanese Character for Satori (Enlightenment)

This book is an Initiation into the vast possibilities of You,
An Initiation into the Truth of who you really are
and what Reiki means in your unfolding Path.
The intention of this book is to free you
to become Reiki.

Read with your heart and not your rational mind.
Contemplate rather than internally debate.
The intention of this writing is not merely to instruct you
but to empower you
to go beyond the normal constructs of your mind
and for the light of understanding to shine within you
and outwith you.
This book is a Transmission
It is my deep and profound connection
with Reiki shared with you.

Mynavati

Let's Begin

Embodiments of Divine Love!
Sri Sathya Sai Baba

You are Reiki. You have always been Reiki. You will always be Reiki. Your discovery of Reiki and your Path of Reiki is a voyage of realisation which takes you beyond mind questions to the heart of what and who this really means. There is no need to ask "What is Reiki?" Ask instead, "Who am I that is Reiki?"

In Truth, you, we, are completely perfect and Whole but this is a difficult concept to take on board in this duality we call life, this split existence comprised of interrelated dualities filled with longings and suffering, a habitat that does not feel Whole at all.

Yet, somewhere under the rubble of rubbish and illusions, You are there—golden and shining. Reiki is your key to unearth You that is always in Truth, that is never separate, that is One with all that is. Reiki is your connection to You in all and all in you. It is your connection to the One unconcerned by sickness and unhappiness, untouched by a state of separateness.

Some may never know that they are disconnected from their true self. They may not know that they are so wondrous. They may know nothing other than the parameters of their daily lives and its dreams. But when one meets with Reiki one is ready to go beyond this. One is ready for the Journey towards the Mystery of Self, where there is no need to try, where there is no need to find anything... where one realises that we have everything that is needed here and now.

Does this mean that you are meant to heal others? Not necessarily. Does this mean that you are meant to be a Reiki Master? In the deepest sense of the meaning, you already are! The question is how to wake up and remember this Truth. Does this mean that you are meant to become famous and rich? You are already deeply blessed and filled with an abundance beyond material gain.

What does it mean if Reiki finds you? I believe it means that you are ready to expand your perceptions of yourself and your world. It means that you are now ready to begin the steps to a very special freedom... from the worldly prison that envelopes you and ordinarily propels you.

I believe that you are ready to seek the Divine Mystery that is you. The you that is Reiki and the Reiki that is you. The you that is Prema Swarupa, an embodiment of Divine Love.

1

Reiki

All attraction is Self to Self

H. W. L. Poonja (Papaji)

Reiki is not the beginning or the end result. It is not a thing, a technique that can be captured and used as a means to an end. You cannot be taught Reiki and you cannot be taught to be a healer that heals people. These are the first illusions you need to let go of.

Can you capture the Sky and use it? Can you capture the immensity of someone's heart and use it? Reiki is not what you can use, it is Who You Truly are and Who You Truly are in union with all that is. If you are attracted to Reiki, it is the attraction of Self to the Greater Self, the You that is One with everything and everyone.

Reiki is sometimes merely a prompt, a nudge, to one's often, sometimes unaware, uncomfortableness. But in essence, Reiki is your code to decipher and unravel the amazing mystery of You and everything that is. Reiki will come to you when you are ready to grow out of yourself, when the chrysalis of a smaller you, a smaller world, can no longer support your tight, itchy squashed being and it splits and you are ready to emerge. You have no choice. Reiki is a word that means much, much, more. It is one word, one way, amongst many unique ways, that leads one home to their True Self. When it is your time, the way for you will come to you and you will take the necessary step. It will not even feel like a choice and it isn't.

2

Universal Life Force Energy

A human being is a part of the whole called by us universe
Albert Einstein

Reiki is known as Universal Life Force Energy. This has become a cliché. Reiki healers say it all the time. But what do they mean? As long as we talk about Reiki as a 'thing" we limit it to something, to a perception, an object, rather than the great mystery of the subject. When it is something, it ceases to be everything. What does Universal mean? What is Life Force Energy? These are to be reflected on, contemplated, encountered, discovered… Realised.

Healers as well as Reiki healers frequently refer to themselves as healing practitioners who channel healing energy to others. Their intentions are sincere. But when we identify ourselves as the channel for healing energy, we claim the responsibility and we limit. We make an offering of crumbs rather than offering the glorious cake from which the crumbs have come.

Rather, let us make conscious, that we are not separate from anyone or any aspect of creation, that there is no doer doing and nothing is being done. There is no one fixing, or in a position to fix. There is no one stronger than another. The Reiki practitioner and another in a healing relationship is a joining of the Truth of the Heart in union with the Truth of the Heart. You are Universal Life Force Energy. The other is Universal Life Force Energy. You are each Universal Life Force Energy. Universal Life Force Energy is Divine Love, is God. All that is You and Another is Universal Life Force Energy, is Divine Love, is God. In this sacred space of Unity, True Healing happens.

3

Initiation

Ready to Receive the Ritual of the Key

Mynavati

We are each in relative stages of slumber in this world we call home. But this home is temporary and is not our permanent abode and when we awaken, we realise this in the same way we awaken from a night dream to another reality, the reality you find yourself in. When we arise from our slumber enough, we are ready to receive the keys to further awakening.

Every spiritual tradition that has ever been and is now has a system of Initiation, a ritualised ceremony which enables the beginning of something new, something secret from before. A rite of passage that potentially speeds the spiritual awakening of the aspirant to know something they could not know before. It is a step, intentionally taken, that facilitates the further steps as yet unknown and unrecognisable in a new reality. Trust is essential. Surrender is necessary to receive the key to the Source of one's power of potential. A potential that cannot yet be understood but is believed to be true.

And so you become an Initiate, ready to receive a transference of something beyond your imagination. A power that will transform you. It is a birth and a death, for this rite of passage takes you beyond who you thought you were and births you into who you are ready to be. Spiritually it is an awakening. An awakening that will ultimately lead to many stages of realisation until you are fully awake and the slumber is no more.

The Transmissional Right of Passage in Reiki is through Attunements, and these are given at each Reiki level. Four Attunements are given at Reiki 1, two Attunements are given at Reiki 11 and one final Attunement is given at Reiki Master level.

During the Attunements the Reiki student receives direct transmission from the Reiki Master and is aligned to the Divine depth and meaning of the symbols used in Reiki. The Reiki Symbols ignite and empower Reiki within the Reiki aspirant.

Attunements are the Divine Nucleus of Reiki training. They are the series of Initiations that amplify and open a Reiki aspirant's energy to Universal Life Force. Creating a purification and an amplification of their entire being on all levels. This triggers a process of cleansing, physically, emotionally, mentally and spiritually, which will last for at least 21 days. (The Spiritual significance of 21 is explained in more detail in the next Chapter). As one's energy expands, obstacles in the way to that expansion, ready, or waiting to be removed are easily purified.

Contrary to some beliefs, Reiki Attunements are not given to open and empower a Reiki participant's energy in order to make them a healer. The Laying on of Hands, of Healing, is a Divine branch, is a great boon from the blessings of Universal Wholeness but is not the main intention of Reiki. All Initiations, Attunements, Empowerments are a Rite of Passage in Reiki to help the Reiki aspirant connect with and to remember who they really are: Universal Life Force. They are to Initiate you on your Spiritual Path towards this realisation. From this Source of Truth within you, from this wealth of spiritual connection, spontaneous and intentional healing blessings can be shared.

Reiki 1 level Attunements, in the main, result in a deepening physical purification as well as degrees of mental and emotional purification that the Reiki participant is ready for. Reiki level 11 Attunements result in an amplification of mental and emotional purification. The Reiki Master Attunement is a deepening Spiritual opening and resultant purification.

4

Transmission

God Uniting with God.
Divine Love uniting with Divine Love

Mynavati

The words in this book, are a transmission into Reiki. The transmission comes from the energy of the words and my relationship with them; a relationship beyond words. A feeling, a happening, a momentum that is present and is shared with you in each word I write. This is present each time you connect with the word Reiki, the feeling of Reiki, the expression of Reiki, the understanding of Reiki, until you increasingly Realise you are Reiki.

The quality, the power, the immensity of transmission cannot be understood rationally or intellectually. It is a miracle and as such we should not even try to understand it. We should merely accept it and flow with it, as a gentle Divine river entering you and flowing through you. All you need do is let go, float, swim, let yourself be enveloped and filled with its miraculous energy.

A transmission permeates every level of you and every little particle of you. It has no beginning and no end. It flows to you and through you and beyond. Let your mind go, for a transmission is a language beyond the ego, beyond the mind.

A transmission is a Divine happening, beyond the rational mind and there the Truth of the Master is Divinely given. This is not the same as influence or suggestion. Transmission is a gift, given by Divine Love through Divine Love to Divine Love using the language of the Heart. It can manifest as a sudden blaze of understanding or a gradual blossoming, like the unfolding of the petals of a lotus to the light of the sun in slow motion.

Be open. Trust. You can receive nothing you are not ready for. You cannot be hurt through a transmission and it cannot be too much for you. You will receive only what you can accept, consciously and subconsciously, you will receive what resonates with you. What is being offered is what you are ready to receive.

Remember that you are not receiving anything that is not true to you, it is not more than you: it is you.

Divine Power can be shared but cannot be removed. No one has more Divine Power than another. All the Divine Power that Is, is within you and not outside you. During empowerments, you are awakened to a level that you are ready for and able to integrate on all levels of you. What you are not able to receive from within you patiently waits until the most perfect time for you.

Your trust in your Reiki Master, the purity of your relationship with them is crucial in receiving transmission. Your receptivity will be heightened the more unarmoured, the more receptive and open you are. This sacred rapport creates a Divine porthole for Divine energy to flow between you and for you to receive all that the Reiki Master reflects, which is yours and which you are now ready to receive.

Satori or enlightenment is an ultimate transmission, Truth igniting Truth. Usui's Satori or Spiritual Rebirth is said to have happened in March 1922, having fasted, chanted and meditated for twenty-one days. He felt the transmission through the Crown, the Divine awakening the Divine. This is the first rediscovery of a Reiki attunement that we know of.

Usui fasted, chanted and meditated for twenty-one days before his Satori. You can also prepare for your Reiki Attunements so that you can receive the transmission as purely and as clearly as possible. And so Reiki Masters generally recommend a cleansing period of a minimum of 3 days and preferably 21 days before the Reiki Attunement and transmissions. You will be asked to avoid heavy foods, (meat) alcohol, tobacco and such like as well as include more reflective meditative time. This prepares your being to be energetically ready to receive the transmissions towards a deeper, more real you.

I ask Reiki aspirants to continue their cleansing time after each level of Reiki for a period of 21 days.

What is so special about 21? We have 5 outer senses, 5 inner senses, five elements and 5 sheaths, which number 20 in total. The 21st day, signifies the 21st part of your being which is now able to integrate the culmination of grace from the period of Empowerment and cleansing throughout all the levels of you. The manifested Grace of the 21st day flows through the entire being, integrating, empowering and awakening.

Footnote:

5 outer senses: touch, hearing, vision, taste and smell.

5 inner senses: imagination, insight, inspiration, instinct and intuition.

5 elements: earth, water, air, fire and space

5 sheaths: Anamaya Kosha is the physical body, Pranamaya Kosha is prana, (Universal energy which flows in and around the body), Manomaya Kosha is the mind, Vinjanamaya Kosha is the psyche, Anandamaya Kosha is the bliss body (when in a state of dreamless sleep and Samadhi)

5

Symbols
Part One

All forms are symbols. Even the human body is a symbol

Mynavati

Our beings connected with symbols as a way of understanding long before language. The Egyptian Book of the Dead is told in pure imagery and symbols. Stone circles, cave paintings, show how human beings have the deepest need to seek and to find meaning, to explore, to go beyond limitations of the mind through symbolic imagery. The most ancient spiritual traditions to present times use highly evolved symbolism in their rituals, prayers and transmissions. Usui's Reiki is most assuredly influenced deeply by the symbols used in Buddhism.

Symbols speak with us on the deepest level. They bypass the mind and speak to our hearts directly. They resonate with us on a cellular level and they have the power to communicate with us, to heal us, to transform us and take us beyond the limitations of the rational mind.

When we relate to our world as symbolic this allows us to go beyond the object and its worldly meaning and connect with something much deeper and greater, outwith the limitation of the meaning of the word itself. A symbol evokes in us a deeper meaning. It directly transmits to the soul to sprout and will sprout like a seed into something unimaginable and Divine. It is a key to the subconscious and the unconscious mind that takes us on a journey beyond the rational mind to the Divine mind which is filled with Awareness.

A symbol can be a word, a movement, an object, an idea. A symbol contains meaning beyond form. It speaks to us multi-dimensionally, reaching far beyond the word, object or idea. It evokes an awakening within us as we alchemically unite with its energy and power and we become changed by the knowledge and awareness of it. A symbol transforms our thinking and opens doorways within us, pathways within us that explode our thought limitations.

Because symbols reach beyond the constructs of the limited mind they are used in ritual, initiations and transmissions. They have the power to transform and redirect our more primal and instinctive nature. A white dove is not just a bird. It is a symbol of peace. And this symbol mysteriously, Divinely, interacts with us and helps us to feel peace and express peace, to be at peace, to share peace... Look at the symbol of a ring? Its symbol is so meaningful and so powerful that Tolkien used the symbol of the ring to write his incredible epic, The Lord of the Rings. Here, the ring is not just symbolically a symbol of devotion and love, Tolkien uses the ring figuratively to change and transform as the story continues, corrupting, enslaving those all but the purest as symbolised by Frodo. This shows us how collectively and personally potent a symbol can be and how its energy and meaning organically changes as the mind and perception changes. A wedding ring is the sign of an accepted bond to one who is happily married but can be a symbol of enslavement to another who is in an unhappy marriage.

Symbols are subjective as well as collective. They are multi-dimension and multi-level. They are the bridge between the mind and the Divine and we use this wondrous Divine flyover in Reiki. In your Reiki Attunements the symbols come in the form of images, words, gestures and thoughts.

Usui's Traditional Reiki Symbols are 4 and we will explore these in Part 2. In Reiki, each symbol is a doorway to a particular state of being and understanding in relation to Universal Wholeness. This connection and understanding unifies all people initiated into and practicing Reiki into a Collective Energy of Reiki Consciousness which is more unifying and supersedes the different Reiki traditions that have sprung up since Reiki was introduced to the West.

The Reiki Symbols are multi-level and alive containing hidden keys that steadily open doors to increasing awareness and Truth as one is energetically ready. They have been and are great teachers to me for which I am deeply grateful. Over many years, the Reiki Symbols transmitted to me have been an endless treasure chest filled with gems of deepening awareness, transmissions, insights and transformation.

Symbols

Part Two

Hidden Jewels

Here, I invite you to join with me in sharing the sacred power of each Reiki Symbol. I will give you the name and the meaning of each symbol but not their symbolic form. I do this because it is important that you seek their full Initiation and transmission face to face, heart to heart, with a Reiki Master that you feel drawn to and feel spiritually connected with rather than attempting to connect to a form drawn on paper and presented in a book.

The forms of each symbol will be subconsciously imparted to you through reading this book and through our naming of them and understanding of their energies. When you are initiated into Reiki 1, you will receive the empowerment of the Reiki Symbols subconsciously through a series of powerful rituals. When initiated into Reiki 11 and Reiki Master levels the symbols will be shared with you on a conscious level and as well as naming the symbols, you will be guided how to draw them, how to use them and how to increasingly empower your connection with them.

If you have not yet been initiated, it is important that the forms of the Reiki Symbols remain secret and sacred to you until you are ready to receive their empowerment through a physical and psychic transmission. If you are already initiated into Reiki 11 and Reiki Master level, I hope that these writings are helpful and inspiring to your already developing Reiki understanding.

There are many Reiki books available with the symbols printed in them. But the symbols are meaningless without their Divine activation through transmission and physical Attunements. Here I hopefully assist with the transmission of a deeper understanding of Reiki. These writings can be used by those seeking to explore and connect with Reiki or those already Initiated who wish to enhance their understanding. Later, when you are ready, you will receive the Reiki Initiations and you will learn how to interact with the forms of these meanings, how to use them, how to respect them and how to keep them sacred.

In respect of the sacredness of This Path, I happily share the meanings of the Reiki Symbols and their names as transmitted to me at my own Reiki Initiations and beyond to allow their complete mystery to unravel, to unfold within you. When you are ready, this opening will lead you to the fullness of your

Initiation with form and meaning with a Reiki Master of your choice.

I was Initiated into four Reiki Symbols, called:

Choku Rei

Hon Sha Ze Sho Nen

Sei Hei Ki

and

Dai Ko Myo

After many years, I directly received the transmission of a further Reiki Master symbol whose Form I will give to you as we progress through the Divine meaning of the Reiki Symbols. This additional symbol embodies for me the protective and holding energy of a Divine Umbrella for Reiki, its Spiritual Path and Healing Practice. A powerful healing symbol which protects and increasingly guides towards the true meaning and practice of Reiki for all sincere Reiki Practitioners: The symbol and form of **The Medicine Buddha**.

6

Choku Rei

(Cho-koo-ray)

I Demand the Power of the Universe

Reiki

In Reiki one, you are subliminally initiated into the sacred power of the Reiki Symbols. In Reiki 11, the form of the symbols and how to draw them are revealed to you. **Choku Rei** is usually the first symbol that is taught in Reiki 11, when Reiki Symbols are made conscious and can be seen and understood and interacted with.

The power of the Universe is synonymous with the power of God. God and Universe is One and is never separated from us. When there is a feeling of separation, of distance from Divinity, from God, it is our mind which is separated, distanced through spiritual sleep, attachment and mind turbulences.

In Reiki 11, when we are introduced to the form and full power of the Reiki Symbols, we now have to take personal responsibility in our interaction and usage of them, to making them conscious within us, to having right Intention and honouring the deepening power of our awareness as our consciousness expands. It is important that we make conscious what we do with our power. In everything we do and say, do we act from our heart, for the good of all beings or merely for the good of our own self?

We invoke a Divine command when we say **Choku Rei**. But what does this command really mean? Some call this command, Put the Power Here, or Increase the Power amongst other commands. I was taught I Demand the Power of the Universe, which I greatly like and resonate with for there is no ambiguity. There is no manipulation of the command under the veil of more diffuse or acceptable words. This command is clear and it is powerful. But let us look at what it really means.

Importantly, there is no reference to past or future in this directive. It is a command anchored in the Now. The Power of the Universe is God. And so when we invoke this symbol we invoke God, Who, while containing all time is not confined to linear time, cyclic time or space; God is present in The Eternal Now.

How can you demand God to be present? Can you demand a higher authority beyond you to do as you will? In Truth, you cannot demand anyone or anything outside of yourself, to do anything you wish or will. But you can wake up. You can wake up to That which is within you which is God. You can demand that you awaken to the power within you here and now... And this is really what this symbol means. **Choku Rei** is the symbolic key to awaken you, to ignite God within you, to command the Divinity within you to bring you to the awareness of your Divine Power, Now. How can this command mean anything else when God is One with you and you are One with God? How can it mean anything else when you are One with God and all that is.

When you invoke God within you, you invoke the power of Divinity that is contained within you. You wake up and claim your Divine Power, Now. Not tomorrow. Not next week or next month or when you feel we are ready or when you think you are ready or when you think you have the time. You claim this Divine power now and in this Now, you focus, you connect, you are aware and you are available for the God within and outwith you. You connect to the awareness that the power of the Universe is completely available to you now and always, that it is part of you. That, this Power is who you truly are.

Choku Rei is a light switch of Power. The more you name it and understand its meaning, the more you draw the symbol when you are Initiated into its energy, the more the connection to this Power, to God, will increase and expand. **Choku Rei** brings you home to the power that is within you and outwith you. The power which is essentially who you are and which is essentially who everyone is. This is the true meaning of Protection, which **Choku Rei** is often believed to be.

When you are focussed, when you are connected, when you are in awareness, you are naturally, automatically connected to your Divine Power and are protected in ways that can be understood as well as ways in which you are yet to understand. Power is neither good nor bad but the way in which we use power, our intention, is a choice. It is a choice between good and bad, wisdom and ignorance and unconditional love and desire. **Choku Rei** asks us to use our power of intention for goodness, for awareness, for kindness, for wisdom. In actuality, one cannot use **Choku Rei** for bad. It just does not respond. It does not work. Simply, when our choices are negative and impure, we just can't connect to the Divine Power within us. No matter how much we command we will be unable to access the Source we seek.

The Power of **Choku Rei**, of the God within us and outwith us, of Divinity, is immeasurably good and cannot be used for evil. It is indefinable and yet tangible. God is personal and God is non-personal. God contains everything. God is eternal. God is Love. God is **Choku Rei**. When you connect with pure Love all the power necessary for that Love to flow within you and outwith you will be present

Choku Rei:

Protects
Cleanses
Empowers
Increases
Improves
Expands
Reflects
Activates
Ignites
Heals
and
Magnifies

In connecting with **Choku Rei**, you acknowledge all the above and more. There is no need to recite these qualities or try to remember them. The symbol of **Choku Rei** embodies the power and expressions of these qualities and as you use the symbol, as you draw it and/or recite its name, you are in relationship with its Power and its wisdom and it will pervade through every cell of your being.

I have been deeply inspired to not use particular Reiki Symbols for a specific outcome. It

I believe that it is not for me to decide what is best for another. It is not for me to decide what is best for me. It is not for me to decide how the symbol should work. We are interacting here with a Living Divine Power and this unlimited power knows what is needed and why. And so if I wish to connect with the Protection of **Choku Rei**, I do so consciously, but I surrender the outcome of that protection to Divine Will and Love for the good of all concerned.

In a Reiki-healing connection, between two people, one is required to be as present as possible to another in the healing relationship, to be completely with them, while removing oneself out of the way from what one thinks is needed or needing to happen. When we let go doer-ship, a beautiful sacred place of healing manifests, which one can immerse oneself into and let go.

Reiki, Universal Life Force, is the love between one and another in a healing relationship.   There is the trust and the surrender that whatever the one asking for healing requires will happen according to the wisdom and healing of Divine Love, the wisdom and healing of Universal Wholeness, the wisdom and healing of God. The wisdom and healing of Reiki.

Why would one limit Divine Power, Universal Life Force by the limitations and specifications of one's own mind?

In a healing connection and relationship with myself or another, I do not use one symbol alone, even if that symbol seems to be a major key to the conditions requiring healing that are manifesting.   I use all four symbols in a particular sequence. A Reiki 11 practitioner will use the three symbols they learn in a particular sequence. As a Reiki Master I use four symbols.   All symbols are an aspect of the Whole.   Each are elements connecting us to Universal Wholeness and so why would I wish to split these elements, when the aim is the wisdom and power of Universal Wholeness?   This sequence is laid out in a following chapter.

Other ways of saying, **I Demand the Power of the Universe** are:

I ask God to be present Here and Now

The Power of Reiki is Here and Now

I surrender to the God in me

I claim the Power of the Universe Now

God is Here

Place the Power of the Universe Here

God and I are One in the Presence of Now

Reiki and I are One in the Presence of Now

I am Divine Power Now

Choku Rei contains the energies of:

Power

Connection

Protection

Magnification

Blessings

Sealing

Strengthening

Opening

Closing

Choku Rei is the power containing the mystery of God, Who heals in ways beyond the limitations of our mind and our will and always blesses with the highest good for all concerned.

Choku Rei, Choku Rei, Choku Rei

Here are three examples where **Choku Rei**'s energy is potently healing.   If you are yet to be initiated into Reiki 11 level, use the mantra sound of the name of **Choku Rei**, in the sequence given later in the book, with the mantra sounds of the other Reiki Symbols.   If you are already initiated into Reiki 11 level, or Reiki Master symbols, use **Choku Rei** together with the other symbols you have been initiated into.

   1. **Strengthening Vulnerability**

If you are feeling vulnerable, place the palms of your hands on your belly area over the navel, the right-hand palm over the left hand palm and say the mantra of the symbols internally or aloud three times. Now place the palms of your hands on your heart area, the right-hand palm over the left hand palm and say the mantra of the symbols internally or aloud three times.

If you have been initiated into the Reiki Symbols draw each one in sequence as though with a beam of Pure Light from your Third-Eye. Draw each symbol, imagining each one as large as you can and when complete imagine stepping into the sacred

2. Blessing Someone Through a Photograph, Object or Food

If the object for healing is not too large to hold, place between the palms of your hands, chant the mantra **Choku Rei** with the other Reiki Symbols at least 3 times. Remain with the palms of your hands on the object until you feel you can move on. Finally, say inwardly or aloud, I bless you, I bless you, I bless you.

If you are a practicing Reiki Practitioner, hold or touch the object with one hand and with the hand you write with, energetically draw the Reiki Symbols with the palm of this hand over and a little above the object. When complete, hold the object between both palms of your hands for a few moments and until you feel you can move on. Finally, say inwardly or aloud, I bless you, I bless you, I bless you.

3. Facilitating Plants to Grow

If the plant is in a pot that can be held, place the pot plant between the palms of your hands, chant the sound of the mantra **Choku Rei** gently onto the plant and in sequence with the other Reiki Symbols for at least 3 times. Remain holding the pot plant with the palms of your hands until you feel you can move on. Finally, say inwardly or aloud, I bless you, I bless you, I bless you.

If the plant/tree is outdoors and is too large or difficult to hold between your hands, be with the plant/tree for a little while in quiet peace connecting with Universal Life Force Energy and chant the sound of the mantra **Choku Rei**, for the plant/tree inwardly or aloud in sequence with the other Reiki Symbols named in this book. Finally, before you move on, say inwardly or aloud, I bless you, I bless you, I bless you.

If you are a Reiki Practitioner, touch the plant gently with one hand and with the hand you write with, energetically draw **Choku Rei** and the Reiki Symbols in sequence with the palm of this hand over/in the direction of the plant. When complete hold the pot plant between both palms of your hands for a few moments and until you feel you can move on. Finally, say inwardly or aloud, I bless you, I bless you, I bless you.

If you are a Reiki practioner and the plant/tree is outdoors and is too large or difficult to hold between your hands, be with the plant/tree for a little while in quiet peace connecting with Universal Life Force Energy and from an imagined beam of Light from your Third-Eye towards the plant/tree, draw Choku Rei in sequence with the symbols you have received during Initiation reciting their names. Finally, before you move on, say inwardly or aloud, I bless you, I bless you, I bless you.

7

Hon Sha Ze Sho Nen

(Hon-Shah-Shay-Show-Nen)

The Buddha in Me Sees The Buddha in You

Reiki

Hon Sha Ze Sho Nen is usually the second symbol taught in Reiki 11. **Choku Rei** claims the Divine Power intrinsic in Universal Wholeness and **Hon Sha Ze Sho Nen** enables the Divine Power to be recognised within oneself and in another, in all others. When we do this, we connect deeply and limitlessly. Awareness is timeless and from this deep awareness beyond time and space we are present to our true self and that very same self in others.

This second Reiki Symbol, beyond time and space, is a Divine Bridge, an inner channel that supersedes and overrides any obstacles or distances between our self and another, between our self and all others and between the levels within us. For when we truly see, when we really grasp how That which is so precious within us is the very same in another, in all others, the whole world changes for us. How can it not? This awareness is the foundation of the concept of Wholeness.

Many try to limit what they fear and imagine as Wholeness, they want to stay self-centred. This leads nowhere but to the magnification of one's own limitations and imprisonment. And it's a lie. Regardless of whether you believe yourself to be separate or an essential part of the Whole, you are Universal Life Force Energy, you are God! And God is not limited. God is not the selection of one person against another person… God is you and him and her. God is everyone, every sentient being and manifestation of Creation.

Your God is not different from my God or another's God. Maybe we interact with our God differently, name our God differently, express our Devotion differently, but it's the same God, the very same God in you and in me and in all others.

The only part of us that is separate, that feels to be apart, that feels different, is a mind that is spiritually distanced from its true connection.

On the profoundest level, **Hon Sha Ze Sho Nen**, is the recognition of the Universal Wholeness of all Life.

Universal Wholeness:

Transforms and contains

Mirrors and reflects

Is One and yet has multiple perfect reflections of Itself

Is illusory and is filled with Space

Is filled with Divine Love and is created by Divine Love

Is Everything

Is Cosmic Reality

Is That which transcends Duality

Is That which transcends time, distance and space

Cosmic Reality is phenomenal. It is undifferentiated. It is Whole. It is One and not two. When your inner eyes open, when the Truth in you sees the Truth in another and you go beyond duality, you will experience Creation transcendentally and not phenomenally. Your experience will not be relative but Absolute. You will see Who you truly are and You in All and All in You. This is the true meaning of **Hon Sha Ze Sho Nen**.

Ways in which **Hon Sha Ze Sho Nen** can be said:

Love in me recognises Love in you

The Divine in me sees the Divine in you

You and I are One

You are Me and I am You

I see You

You and I are the One and the same Source

You and I are the embodiment of Divine Love

God in me sees God in you

My Light honours your Light

Hon Sha Ze Sho Nen, having no limitations of distance, connects you to all no matter how far, how distant.

Distance is a concept our mind creates in Duality. It is an idea and an actuality of separation in Duality. Without Duality the measure of how far one thing is from another is a nonsense. In Duality it is an illusion. In physics, action at a distance is the concept that an object can be moved, changed or otherwise affected without being physically touched by another object. In quantum physics this is called Entanglement where if you observe a particle in one place, another particle, even one light-years away will instantly be affected and change its properties. In Science this is identified as a mysterious communication, but Spiritually, it is a very simple explanation of the vast subject of interdependence and sameness, Oneness and in particular of the meaning of **Hon Sha Ze Sho Nen.**

There is no distance where there is recognition. The Buddha in me Sees the Buddha in you has no boundary, has no distance or separation. It reflects a deep connection on all levels, no matter how distant one seemingly is from another in Duality. It reflects a deep connection beyond our ideas of Duality.

Distance is illusory. Physically we can be in close proximity to another and yet be and feel worlds apart. We can be physically distant from another and yet feel incredibly connected.

Hon Sha Ze Sho Nen reflects the transcendent energy of time and space and perfect energy bridge for Distant Healing. All you need is intention. All you need is Love. If you wish to have a healing relationship connection with another, write down their name, their suffering on a piece of paper and hold this paper against your heart, the right-hand palm over the left hand palm and be with them. Recite the mantra sound of **Hon Sha Ze Sho Nen** in sequence with the other Reiki Symbols sounds given in these writings at least three times then let go and remain in union for a little while and until you feel ready to move on.

Do not try to limit your focus to one particular aspect of their suffering or part of the body. Place your awareness on the immensity and compassion of the heart, surrendering to Divine Love which knows the perfect solution for the best outcome on all levels

When initiated into the Reiki Symbol forms, use **Hon Sha Ze Sho Nen** in sequence with the other Reiki Symbols you are empowered to use in your connection to distant healing.

Remember that each symbol energetically supports the others and connects us to Universal Life Force and its relationship with Wholeness. When used in sequence with the other symbols, **Hon Sha Ze Sho Nen** creates a Universal Bridge that facilitates the energy of Universal Wholeness, of Divine Love.

Initiated Reiki Practitioners from level 11 learn how to draw the symbols. Always use the palm(s) of your hand to draw the symbol, or the Third Eye, the energy point between the eyebrows, imagining a beam of light radiating out from your inner eye.

The palms of your hands contain energy centres (Chakras) directly connected to the Heart Chakra. This means that they are an expression of your Divine Heart. When laying the palms of your hands directly onto self or another, your heart's energy is activated and flows from the Heart's Wellspring of loving-kindness, through the palms of your hands. The palms of your hands contain the energy of giving and receiving and the more you use the palms of your hands with intention and the awareness of their connection to your heart, the stronger their energy centres will open and the more powerful the healing of Compassion will flow through them.

This is far more powerful, expansive and healing than drawing with your finger or fingers as I have seen some Reiki Practitioners do. Try this. Try writing your name in the space before you using your index finger, or any finger if you wish or all your fingers together and then try writing your name in space using the palm of your hand. You will tangibly experience the difference.

Another test you can do is by connecting with a vulnerable part of your body. Place one or more fingers on this area and examine how you feel. Now, instead place the palms of your hands over this area for a few minutes and compare the difference.

The Third-Eye is also powerful for drawing the Reiki Symbols in space before someone or over the name of someone. The Third-Eye is the entry into the vastness and connectivity of the inner eye and its limitless power. The Third-Eye is a place of energy within us that can unify us and our splitness, our disharmony into a place of balance and harmony. When we are clear and in balance, our focus, intention, clarity and will is empowered and we can connect with Universal Life Force and Reiki purely and powerfully.

Examples of Distant Healing

1. Connecting with a Photograph

Place a photograph of someone you wish to have a healing relationship connection with and place this photograph in an envelope. Hold this envelope to your heart, your right-hand palm over your left hand palm and recite the mantra sound of **Hon Sha Ze Sho Nen** in sequence with the sounds of the other Reiki Symbols. Stay in this healing connection until you feel ready to move on.

When Initiated at Reiki 11 level, please do as above but with the addition of drawing the **Hon Sha Ze Sho Nen** symbol, in sequence with the other Reiki Symbols, over the envelope containing the person's name or photograph you wish to connect with in a healing relationship. Chant the sound of **Hon Sha Ze Sho Nen** and the other Reiki Symbols names in sequence.

2. Accessing Different Levels of You

Hon Sha Ze Sho Nen is a key energy of the Reiki Symbols that facilitates connection with different levels of you. This symbol overrides the distance between your subconscious and conscious mind and its obstacles and resistances.

Use a photograph of yourself and write your name on a piece of paper. Place in an envelope between the palms of your hands or place on your heart area with your right-hand palm over your left hand palm. Recite the mantra sound and meaning of **Hon Sha Ze Sho Nen** in sequence with the other Reiki Symbols and their sounds. Clearly connect with your intention for clarity, for insight into what needs to be brought to light, for balance and healing. Stay in this place of meditation until you feel you wish to move on.

When Initiated in Reiki 11 or Master Level, do as above but also draw **Hon Sha Ze Sho Nen** on the outside of the paper in sequence with the other Reiki Symbols you have been initiated into, connecting with their meanings and reciting their mantra sounds.

To access your subconscious mind and what is motivating you, place your photograph and or name in a small envelope drawing all the Reiki Symbols on the outside of the envelope including **Hon Sha Ze Sho Nen** and place under your pillow with the intention of wishing to understand or access consciously, through insights and or dreams, your subconscious fears, wounds, motivations and habits which are creating obstacles for you. On waking, immediately write down any thoughts or dreams you remember and reflect on these over the next few days. If you are not yet Initiated into Reiki, write the names of the Reiki symbols in sequence and continue as above.

3. Healing Different Ages of Yourself

Hon Sha Ze Sho Nen reaches beyond time and space as well as distance. Heal different personal experiences and ages by placing a photograph of yourself at a particular age or by writing down your name and the age you wish to heal. Place in an envelope, writing the name of **Hon Sha Ze Sho Nen,** in sequence with the names of the other Reiki Symbols, on the outside of the envelope. Hold this envelope to your heart surrendering your healing to the power of Divine Love, your right-hand palm over your left-hand palm.

If you are Initiated into the Reiki Symbols from Reiki 11 level, do as above but in addition, draw the Reiki Symbols as well as their energy names.

You may wish to consecutively go through every year of your life since birth. You can do this daily or if this feels too much or too fast for you, each week.

With any healing relationship connection to self or another, always examine your intentions, try not to limit, surrender to Universal Life Force Energy, to Divine Love, to God. Let go. Trust, that the healing will be absolutely perfect and be the best for all concerned. Beginning and ending any Healing Practice with Thy Will not my will for the good of all concerned.

8

Sei Hei Ki

(Say-Hay-Key)

I have The Key

Reiki

Sei Hei Ki is the third Reiki Symbol given in Reiki 11 Initiations.

This symbol looks like a key and it is a key. Some call it God and man are One, or Earth Meeting the Sky or some call it simply harmony. These words reflect the deeper meaning of the meeting between Divinity and humanity, between the Divine and the Human and this is the Key... the Key to Awakening, to Initiation, to the freedom of Spiritual equanimity and Divine wisdom.

It has been summarized as the emotional/mental symbol, but it is much, much, more than this. Yes, it can be used to help balance emotional and mental disturbances, to purify, to heal emotional wounds, but let us imagine what can happen when we have the key to do this and more? Here, we have the potential to transform, to evolve past our conditioning and to move past worldly entrapments.

Sei Hei Ki contains the Key to**:**

Awareness

Understanding

Transformation

Mental, Emotional and Spiritual Balance

Focussing of the mind

Empowering the mind and memory

Easing anxiety

Facilitate sleep

Diffuse and release addiction and addictive behaviour

Let go and move on from negative energies

Bring into harmony

Remember dreams

Awaken your being to meet with God/Divinity

Sei Hei Ki opens the doorway through a closed, habitual mind caught in subconscious patterns that hurt us and influence us to continue in ways that are unhealthy, limiting and negative.

Our subconscious mind drives and influences our conscious mind and as to whether or not we have emotional, mental and spiritual balance. Using the Key, **Sei Hei Ki**, we bring into manifestation the awareness of choice and how through our conscious efforts and good intentions we can change our mind and consequently our life for the benefit of self and all around us. When caught in habits, we have little choice. But evedn accessing some awareness that we have these patterns is a big step forward on the path towards freedom from them.

This is the key to unlocking negativities and patterns, to making them conscious and it is through our conscious awareness and our good intentions that change can happen. It is through awareness that we have increased choice. And when we have the freedom of choice we can choose to make positive changes in our lives, as well as benefiting from a clearer and more positive mind. **Sei Hei Ki** is literally the key to balance and heal the mind, thereby healing the emotions sufficiently for us to begin to grow spiritually.

This is a powerful symbol to use to help change your mind patterns, to dissolve Vasanas (habitual tendencies) through the power of positive affirmations.

Our minds are filled with imbalances, negative patterns, crippling desires, fears, cravings and insecurities. These influence and form our perspective of the world as well as the formation of our world, who we befriend, who we marry, who we choose to accept and reject, who we choose to love and who we choose to dislike or even hate.

On the most elevated level, **Sei Hei Ki**, frees our mind towards increasing spiritual growth and awakening.

We can use Affirmations to change specific negative patterns of thoughts into positive thoughts. Once we know how to work with Affirmations and **Sei Hei Ki**, this is an easy tool.

Drawing, reciting **Sei Hei Ki** before and after saying an Affirmation is extremely powerful ritually, potentially opening the mind, to let go, to receive the positive meaning and sounds of a new way of thinking, a new way of being.

Merely just using the sound of the symbol can help, although once initiated you will also mentally draw and visualise the form of the sound and meaning. For now, here is a secret gem, a gateway on how to use the sound of **Sei Hei Ki** with an Affirmation.

Cup your right-hand palm over the Alter Major Chakra, (the protruding bump at the lower back of your head), also called the Occiput, with your left-hand palm lightly touching the crown and repeat **Sei Hei Ki,** followed by your Affirmation, followed by **Sei Hei Ki**. Do this for three times minimum and up to a maximum of 21 times if you feel you need to. Energetically it is like easing a new image, a new positive belief and feeling, effortlessly into your mind.

The Alter Major Chakra is the Chakra energy of our primal self and holds the key to change your patterns on the deepest subconscious level. Located at the back of the head, just above the point where the skull joins the neck is part of the direct conduit of kundalini from the bottom of the spine, where this energy rests, to the flow towards the Crown. This Chakra, links to the Hypothalamus, Pineal and Pituitary glands. It has been referred to as the mouth of God and begins directly at the back of the Third Eye.

Intuition is accessed here, inspiration as well as a primal instinct for safety and protection. More than anything, here, we access the seat of Consciousness. A seat that is an opening... An opening to the mind's transformation, freeing it from the obstruction of Vasana driven thoughts, actions and reactions. Used with **Sei Hei Ki**, its unbeatable...

A Vasana is an underlying psychological-psychic imprint in us, caused by a continual mind-patterning strengthened by repetition. Consequently, this imprint-patterning is compulsed to repeat itself again and again in all kinds of ways. It is a vicious cycle that is hard to break as it embeds itself in our subconscious mind and compels us to retain and strengthen the pattern endlessly.

And so this is your root addiction from which all your other addictions stem. Your root Vasana is your jailor and imprisons you in a limited habitual and often unconscious world.

Using **Sei Hei Ki** and holding the occiput in the way described above for affirmations, you can directly work with the Vasana level and bring to your awareness the habits within you ready to be freed. It is always best to declare something positive rather than something negative and so, if you wish to let go, say a pattern of anxiety for example, you can declare while holding the occiput, the opposite of your negative: the positive. Reciting **Sei Hei Ki** while cupping the occiput with your right-hand palm and lightly touching the crown with your left hand declare I am filled with courage. I am courageous.

Later after Initiation into the form of the symbol, you will also be able to mentally or physically draw over or onto the occiput with your right-hand palm or your third-eye before placing your right-hand palm on the occiput itself.

This ritual can be repeated three to 21 times.

The simplest, most powerful way to lessen the influence and power of a Vasana, is to identify it, name it, witness it, claim it and consciously choose its positive opposite.

Here we use **Sei Hei Ki** to open the lock of an imprisoning Vasana door and once done, increasing understanding can come and the lock can never be secure again no matter how many times it tries to recapture you and imprison you.

Footnote:

Be Happy with Heal, Meditation and Affirmation (Part 3) by Mynavati extensively explores Affirmations and how to use them further, including using the power of 21 repetitions.

Mynavati has written a three-part guide on Vasanas and how to work with them in her website www.mynavati.com

Vasanas Part 1: Cutting the Vasana Tree; Dissolving the Roots

Vasanas Part 2: Treating Vasanas as an Addiction

Vasanas Part 3: Steps of Awareness - Dissolving the Vasana

9

The Master Symbol

Dai Ko Myo

(Die Ko Me Yo)

Let The Great Light Shine

Reiki

During the Reiki Master Level, one is initiated into The Master Symbol **Dai Ko Myo**.

This symbol is a Divine celebration proclaiming, *Let the Great Light Shine.* We travel within from *I demand the Power of the Universe* to the fullness of The Great Light. The culmination of the full expression of the Spiritual and Healing Journey through the passage of each Reiki Symbol is expanding, shining, Radiant Light.

The only true healing is our merging into Light and being One with Light, where there is no you or I, where there is no he or she, where there is no healer and patient, where there is no Godly Deity or Goddess, where there is only One, That which is beyond form, beyond the personal I. The ancient Vedic scriptures term this state of being as Sat-Chit-Ananda.

Sat-Chit-Ananda is:

Awareness, Consciousness, Bliss.

Sat-Chit-Ananda is the subjective experience of the Radiance and the bliss of the ultimate, unchanging Reality. Absolute Reality unlike relative Reality which is based in duality and includes perceptions of you and I, like and dislike, acceptance and rejection, sickness and health.

Absolute non-changing Truth is reflected in Sat-Chit-Ananda. Sat is Truth and is Consciousness free from the distortions created by the mind. It is That which has no separate you, separate witness or separate perception. The culmination of Grace of all the Reiki Symbols merged into One. Wholeness, Oneness, That which Is.

We have the possibility to experience Sat-Chit-Ananda in life because it contains Consciousness (Chit). Because, in spite of Duality we are Consciousness and can experience Sat, can witness, That which is the Absolute, non-changing Truth. Here we experience the True Self, like a beacon of Light, within the darkness of duality, the "I" that fully comprehends. This is not a personal experience. It is an experience of Absolute Reality remembered by the Consciousness within one.

Connecting with the Radiance of **Dai Ko Myo,** you connect with the potential for the total healing of all levels of you and those you connect with. It is like entering a pool of bliss and becoming Bliss Itself, bathing in the Light of Bliss. How can healing not happen? A true healing of body, mind and spirit, of all levels, emotional, mental, psychological and spiritual.

All that manifests, that is created, that is imbalanced and can be healed is born from Ultimate Universal Reality and its healing needs to be from That which is Absolute Reality. Everything else is a band aid: a help, a soother, a superficial temporary remedy. For True Healing to happen, you need to get out of the way, remove yourself from the personality and ego's ideas of how things should be, of what you or the one you are in a healing connection with needs or believes the ways things should be. Let go dear one and submerge into the Radiant Great Light, consciously surrendering to Its Power of Absolute Healing; *Let The Great Light Shine*

The Great Light is:

Divine

Illuminating

Filled with Wisdom

All pervading

Eternal

Enlightened

Filled with Bliss

God Energy

Filled with Divine Love

Filled with Awareness

When one is initiated as a Reiki Master, when one consciously receives the Reiki Master symbol, **Dai Ko Myo,** the seeds of ever-increasing Oneness with Universal Wholeness within you waiting to bloom, will blossom and grow. The seeds will germinate and sprout, as you engage in the ongoing work of Your dedication to your Spiritual Path. This is an ever-increasing unfolding Path towards The Great Light of Reiki and its healing. It is an unfolding growth, that increases your integrity and commitment to Unconditional Love, to Compassion.

During Reiki 1 you are introduced to Reiki and receive four Initiations and transmissions of the Reiki Symbols and their power subconsciously. You are encouraged how to connect with loving-kindness to yourself and others, and how to practice self-healing using hand-placements. These can only be used with others in an informal way.

During Reiki 11, you are Initiated into three of the symbols on a Conscious level. There is the opportunity of a deepening awareness of the understanding of Reiki through understanding the Reiki Symbols and you are encouraged to actively use these in your self-healing and in healing connection relationships with others. As you progress, informal healing connections with others can progress gradually to formal healing connections and times with others.

At Reiki Master level, you receive the transmission and Initiation of the Reiki Master symbol. You are guided how to Initiate and how to engage in the rituals of Transmission and Empowerment in preparation for when Reiki calls you to do so. Most important of all, the potential of your Path to increasing understanding, spiritual growth and wisdom is empowered with an accompanying acceleration in your connection to the power and meaning of Universal Life Force energy, your connection to Divine Love and its sustenance, your connection to Compassion.

You now walk the Path towards an ever-increasing understanding and awareness of Reiki and your Divine fulfilment as a Reiki Participant, Reiki Practitioner and when ready, Reiki Teacher. You now walk the Path to realising the Divine promise of the following Chapter.

10

Medicine Buddha

The Ultimate Healer

*Image courtesy of Medical Centre Thangka,
Gajang Tsawa Khangsten, Mondgod, India*

I was initiated into four Reiki Symbols and I continue this lineage by initiating those who come to me with the same symbols I received. Over time the Reiki Symbolic meanings expanded my awareness and took me beyond my initial connection and understanding of Reiki on a deepening journey into the true nature and meaning of Reiki, of the symbols and of how rather than a technique of Spiritual Healing, Reiki is essentially a powerful non-denominational Spiritual Path. The technique and the practice of hands-on Spiritual Healing stem from the blessings of this Path and is a rare, manifested branch of Reiki Divine Power.

Reiki is Universal Wholeness. Different religions and Spiritual Paths may use different terminologies to explain what this is, but ultimately they will and do, all come to the same conclusion. Universal Wholeness represents the True Self. Non-divisible, timeless, what some would imagine as God, or as Divine Love, Reality as against relative reality or Duality, Buddha mind and so on… This is the place within us that is untarnished and unpolluted by Duality, which is perfect and whole and which is One with everything that is. This is the place that is not personal and controlled by ego but by our Universal self which is Divine. It is our true Divine Nature.

The point here is that when we are initiated into Reiki, we begin with the Journey of the self towards the greater Self and the deeper we journey within us to the True Self, the more we are automatically, spontaneously, purified, aware and compassionately available to others, able to participate in the healing of others if this is what we and Reiki wish.

Reiki is the Path of Compassion and Compassion is the Path of the True Healer containing The Path of the Bodhisattva, whose wish for increasing awareness and wisdom, increasing understanding for the benefit of all, to remove suffering and the causes of suffering of all sentient beings.

As time went on and my relationship with Reiki deepened and expanded, I experienced the direct transmission of a Supreme symbolic energy which contained the essence of and the meaning of Reiki and its symbols as well as the way forward for both Reiki Practitioners and for those initiated as Reiki Masters ad-infinitum.

This symbol is The Medicine Buddha, the Ultimate Healer, The First Doctor, the Healing Guru of all Healing Gurus, the primordial Spiritual Power of all forms of Healing including Reiki.

Although a treasured healing practice in the Mahayana Buddhist Tradition, unlike some Tibetan Buddhist empowerments, the Medicine Buddha Practice and Chant can be used personally for your own healing and for the healing of others, whether you are a practicing Buddhist or not. This is a Power identified and named as The Medicine Buddha, but is not limited to this form. Medicine Buddha is a Universal Symbol of Healing and the Healing Path. And so here, is not the transmission or the introduction to a Buddhist practice but to a Divine Healing Practice, used in various ways and words not only by Tibetan Buddhists, but by other lineages of Buddhism as well as those who are not Buddhists.

I was not initiated into the Medicine Buddha Practice as part of my Initiation as Reiki Master, but I was previously and subsequently initiated into Tibetan Buddhism and received the Medicine Buddha initiation a number of times, as well as the Bodhisattva vows, from living Bodhisattvas in the Tibetan Buddhist Tradition while spending a number of years living with Tibetan Masters. I am not a practicing Buddhist although I continue with a strong connection to many of the Masters and the teachings however I did not consciously make the connection between the energy of Medicine Buddha and Reiki, ridiculous though this seems to me now. It was just not the right time. It was not Reiki's time.

I do not wish to offer you something that should only be given by a particular Tradition and I discussed this many years ago with a revered Tibetan Lama who advised me that if I knew someone, others, who would benefit with my sharing this practice and knowledge I should pass this on. I did not know at the time why he said this to me or what he fully meant, but I do now.

The Medicine Buddha practice and chant is not a secret Initiation. It is available to Buddhists and non-Buddhists no matter which tradition or beliefs they hold. The key to the success of all Spiritual transmissions, to obtaining the power of any Divine practice, is the connection you feel to the Source of that transmission and to your faith and trust in it. If you have faith, if you feel a connection to the Divine energy of the Medicine Buddha, or the Healing Buddha, you have this connection, no matter the name and the form, no matter the tradition and no matter whether you think you deserve it or not.

The Medicine Buddha energy, the doctor who cures suffering using the medicine of His teachings, was noted in Spiritual texts dating back to the 6th century in Japan, and the 7th century in India. It is recorded in both texts that the Medicine Buddha made 12 vows for helping all sentient beings, where He pledged to remove suffering and disease for as long as His vows were needed. This is the only Divine Spiritual Deity in Buddhism believed to cure physical illnesses as well as spiritual. A copy of the hallowed 12 vows from the Medicine Buddha Sutra is outlined at the end of this chapter.

A number of years after my Reiki Master Initiation, I received the Medicine Buddha's Divine Compassion as a direct transmission when in a deep meditative state. The realisations from this transmission expanded over a period of time but from the increasing insights I was in no doubt of the connection between The Medicine Buddha energy and the energy of Reiki Healing. The connection anchored in me when I made conscious the fact that the Medicine Buddha was identified and revered in various lineages of Buddhism as well as in Japanese Buddhism where Usui was a lay monk. I can find no written reference to Usui being connected with or of using the practice of Medicine Buddha but I cannot imagine how, in being a Buddhist lay monk and a healer, that he would not be familiar with the Medicine Buddha and practice or its powerful influence, even though this has not been recorded. This for me was a missing key. A key that brought about the deeper meaning for me of the Reiki Spiritual Path and the Reiki Symbols.

Medicine Buddha symbolises the energy of the eternal Bodhisattva, the true healer, One who is able to reach Nirvana but who remains in duality through the deepest compassion for all who are suffering. In an ancient text, Shantideva explains how the Bodhisattva vow is taken:

Just as all the previous Sugatas, the Buddhas
Generated the mind of enlightenment
And accomplished all the stages
Of the Bodhisattva training,
So will I, too, for the sake of all beings,
Generate the mind of enlightenment
And accomplish all the stages
Of the Bodhisattva training.

And so the Bodhisattva denies Enlightenment and full mergence with the Absolute Reality until every blade of grass is realised.

For a Bodhisattva, the motivation for living, for their life, for breathing, for eating, for healing, is this very wish, the wish to alleviate suffering and the causes of suffering for all sentient beings.

Essentially, this is the Path of Reiki and the Path of Reiki Initiation. This is the Path of Reiki Healers. An Initiation that deepens with the awareness of each consecutive symbol and its meaning. This is the Path of the Reiki Practitioner and the Reiki Master; the Spiritual Path towards the greatest Wisdom and Compassion with the intention to ease the suffering of all beings. This is your Path if you are reading these words and are not running away from them.

Reiki healers of all creeds and nationalities, are not separate from the essence of **Medicine Buddha**. We may appear to be separate but in Truth this essence is within us and when we connect to **The Medicine Buddha** we connect with the blessings intrinsic to The Medicine Buddha's vows. We connect to the Divine essence within and outwith all healers and all forms of healing, through the embodiment of healing compassion intrinsic to Medicine Buddha. **Choku Rei**, I have the Power, **Hon Sha Ze Sho Nen**, with this Power, The Buddha in me sees the Buddha in you. **Sei Hei Ki**, I have the Key to understanding the depths of this awareness leading to **Dai Ko Myo,** Let the Great Light Shine. **The Medicine Buddha** is the Path of the Bodhisattva. The Path of the Bodhisattva is the ultimate Spiritual Path of Reiki and the Reiki Healer.

All the symbols on this Path will interact with you, will open your heart, will deepen your awareness and understanding and will guide your Spiritual growth towards true healing. Healing for self and others. They will lead you on the Path of the Bodhisattva if the wish within you arises to do this.

You may be drawn to try to help physical conditions, mental difficulties, emotional problems, psychic disturbances, all kinds of difficulties, but the deepest healing, the truest healing that can happen is the recognition of the Divinity within self and within others, the meeting of love and unity and the blissful radiant Light of healing that comes from this. **The Medicine Buddha** is for me the final secret transmissional symbol that reveals the seed, the essence and the culmination of all other Reiki Symbols and the revelation of the Reiki Spiritual Path. One cannot heal unless one surrenders oneself to personally healing on all possible levels. To be free of suffering as much as is possible and from the causes of suffering. All true healing comes from being free of desires and expectations and mindful to *not try to heal, your way but Thy way.*

Remember you are on a Path and you will grow. You are not expected to be perfect. You may not feel good enough, or pure enough or clever enough or even physically up to the task. But no one begins the Path as though already arrived.

The Reiki Path will increasingly open your heart to the hearts of all, evolving you into an ever-deepening Compassion for all beings including self. A Path that will lead you towards an increasing awareness and peace. A Path that will lead you to heal yourself and all that you are an intrinsic part of.

Using the Reiki Symbols daily for self and when in a healing connection with self or another, with others, will increasingly purify you and open your mind to progressively deepening your understanding of them. **The Medicine Buddha Practice** and symbol can be your protective umbrella, your safe holding and the guide for your Path as a Healer.

When performing this practice, you are not meant to reach out to an almighty external Great Being or God, who can help you. You are connecting with and awakening the Divine compassionate power within you as symbolised by the form of **Medicine Buddha**, a power that is within you and all beings although often asleep.

Through the ritual of invocation, imagery and sound, you connect with the Divine Energy of the eternal Loving Compassion of numberless beings containing **the Medicine Buddha** power of Healing. You connect with this blessed power within you, you who is part of this Great Consciousness and is indivisible with it.

I give here as much as is possible a simplified non-denominational practice of the Overseer of your Reiki Path; of the energy towards your Spiritual fulfilment and Realisation.

Before we continue, here is an offering of the meaning of **The Medicine Buddha** mantra which we will chant in **The Medicine Buddha Practice**.

Medicine Buddha's mantra:

TAYATA, OM BEKANDZE BEKANDZE
MAHA BEKANDZE BEKANDZE,
RADZA SAMUNGATE
SOHA

Tayata - means it goes like this

Om - primordial sound syllable of all that is created

Bekandze Bekandze - eliminating pain, eliminating pain. The pain of true suffering and the pain of the true causes of suffering

Maha Bekandze Bekandze - maha means great, and so we have the great elimination of pain, the ultimate medicine that eliminates pain on all levels and in all subtleties

Radza - the great king, (of medicine and healing)

Samudgate - vast, endless goodness (surrender to)

Soha - so be it

The Medicine Buddha Practice

Find a quiet place, your sacred space for your meditation. Ensure you are comfortable, sitting with your back straight and not lying down. Surrender yourself to the Buddha, (the enlightened mind), the Dharma (right behaviour and right action) and the Sangha (the good company of your Teacher and those on the same Path as you whether you know them or not).

Connect with your intention. Reflect on why you are doing this Practice. Connect with feelings of loving-kindness, of Compassion for yourself, your loved ones and all beings. Pray that "through this Practice may I and all sentient beings be free from disease, pain and suffering on all levels of our being. May we attain the wisdom to know Peace, Happiness and Compassion for ourselves and all beings. May we realise Divine Love within us and without us."

Invite **The Medicine Buddha** to be with you and imagine, visualize Medicine Buddha sitting around one metre in front of you, elevated to around the height of your forehead, just above the level of your eyes. His body is dark blue in colour, the colour of dazzling lapis lazuli, the colour of His healing. His left hand holds a bowl filled with healing nectar and his right hand holds a powerful medicinal plant. He gazes down at you with immeasurable love, the greatest Love that you have ever felt. He is luminous, his entire body filled with Light, filled with the radiance of Divine Love.

If it is difficult initially to visualise **Medicine Buddha** use an image of him that you feel drawn to, or use the one given at the beginning of this chapter. Believe that **The Medicine Buddha** is present, that you are the recipient of His powerful and profound healing energy. An energy filled with unlimited compassion, unlimited forgiveness, unlimited acceptance, unlimited Love, unlimited healing, radiating from his eyes, from His entire Being

Pray, request, that **Medicine Buddha** removes your suffering and the suffering of all beings. Pray, request, that He removes disease where there is disease, pain where there is pain, that He purifies where there is need of purification, balances where there is need for harmony and grants the blessings of wisdom where there is ignorance.

Visualise **Medicine Buddha** willingly, eagerly, earnestly, responding to your prayers. See Divine nectar from the healing bowl on his lap, radiate and flow to the crown of your head, entering your being, filling you with its potent healing energy. The healing energy flows into every cell of you, filling your entire being, all the levels of you, physically, mentally, emotionally, spiritually. The energy flows so abundantly that you are completely filled by its effulgence and it spills over and gently flows to your loved ones, those you know and care about, those you do not know, whom you will never know, flowing to all sentient beings, in all places, on all levels, in all Creation.

In this everlasting Now, **The Medicine Buddha's** healing power cures you, completely, permanently, from all your suffering and the causes of your suffering. The **Medicine Buddha's** healing power cures all those you care for and love and frees them from their suffering and the causes of their suffering. **The Medicine Buddha's** healing power cures all those you know and those you will never know, all sentient beings and frees them from their suffering and the causes of suffering.

Staying with the wondrous visualisation, with the Divine Healing, recite **The Medicine Buddha's** mantra in Sanskrit for 21 times:

TAYATA, OM BEKADZE BEKADZE
MAHA BEKADZE BEKADZE,
RADZA SAMUNGATE
SOHA

Pronounced as:

TIE-YA-TAR, OM BECK-AND-ZAY BECK-AND-ZAY
MA-HA BECK-AND-ZAY BECK-AND-ZAY
RUN-ZUH SUM-OON-GUT-EH
SO-HA.

When complete, stay in the silence for a few minutes immersed in the power of this powerful healing, feeling the mantra energy flow through your body. Feeling its power flow through every cell of you.

Visualise **Medicine Buddha** slowly disperse into glorious streaming rainbows. Bright colourful rays dissolving further into Radiant Pure White Light... The Light of **Dai Ko Myo**. Let the Great Light Shine eternally for all.

Pray that through this Practice, that you and all beings be free from suffering and the causes of suffering. That you may all be happy and take care of yourselves and one another happily too. Pray that you and all will achieve perfect Oneness with Divine Love and be free to Heal.

The Twelve Vows of the Medicine Buddha upon attaining Enlightenment, according to the **Medicine Buddha** Sutra are:

1. I vow that my body shall shine as beams of brilliant light on this infinite and boundless world, showering on all beings, getting rid of their ignorance and worries with my teachings. May all beings be like me, with a perfect status and character, upright mind and soul, and finally attaining enlightenment like the Buddha.

2. I vow that my body be like crystal, pure and flawless, radiating rays of splendid light to every corner, brightening up and enlightening all beings with wisdom. With the blessings of compassion, may all beings strengthen their spiritual power and physical energy, so that they could fulfil their dreams on the right track.

3. I vow that I shall grant by means of boundless wisdom, all beings with the inexhaustible things that they require, and relieving them from all pains and guilt resulting from materialistic desires. Although clothing, food, accommodation and transport are essentials, it should be utilized wisely as well. Besides self-consumption, the remaining should be generously shared with the community so that all could live harmoniously together.

4. I vow to lead those who have gone astray back to the path of righteousness. Let them be corrected and returned to the Buddha way for enlightenment.

5. I vow that I shall enable all sentient beings to observe precepts for spiritual purity and moral conduct. Should there be any relapse or violation, they shall be guided by repentance. Provided they sincerely regret their wrong-doings, and vow for a change with constant prayers and strong faith in the Buddha,

they could receive the rays of forgiveness, recover their lost moral and purity.

6. I vow that all beings who are physically disabled or sick in all aspects be blessed with good health, both physically and mentally. All who pay homage to Buddha faithfully will be blessed.

7. I vow to relieve all pain and poverty of the very sick and poor. The sick be cured, the helpless be helped, the poor be assisted.

8. I vow to help women who are undergoing sufferings and tortures and seeking for transformation into men. By hearing my name, paying homage and praying, their wishes would be granted and ultimately attain Buddhahood.

9. I vow to free all beings from evil thought and its control. I shall lead them onto the path of light through inculcating them with righteousness and honour so that they will walk the Buddha way.

10. I vow to save prisoners who have genuinely repented and victims of natural disasters. My supreme powers will bless those who are sincere and be freed from sufferings.

11. I vow to save those who suffer from starvation and those who committed a crime to obtain food. If they hear my name

and faithfully cherish it, I shall lead them to the advantages of Dharma and favour them with the best food that they may eventually lead a tranquil and happy life.

12. I vow to save those who suffer from poverty, tormented by mosquitoes and wasps day and night. If they come across my name, cherish it with sincerity and practice dharma to strengthen their merits, they will be able to achieve their wishes.

11

Some Final Words on Reiki,
Reiki Healing and Symbols

You cannot get anything from anyone, from anywhere, that does not belong to you. This includes negativities. So many healers and Reiki Practitioners believe that they can be contaminated with other people's energies when in a healing relationship and that they need to cleanse themselves afterward.

However, if you believe that you are not the *doer*, which is the fundamental premise of Reiki, if you hand yourself over before any healing session and you are *not trying* to obtain a result, there is no-one to be contaminated. There is no one to be the recipient of another's energy. You will be unaffected, protected and remain vibrant. If you become drained and feel vulnerable, it is because you are invested somehow in the healing, in outcomes. Expectations, a need for specific outcomes, a need for validation, will usually result in an emotional reaction within you that will most likely make you tired, angry and feeling unprotected.

Reiki is the most beautiful journey and healer because the hands on-healing is a deep expression of the inner connection to the Absolute Energy of Healing; the Divine Source from whichever form you choose to connect with. Your hands, your energy, your voice, are all marvelous healing extensions of your Divine Heart.

The Reiki Symbols are the most beautiful reflection and expression of your connection to Life Force Energy, to Universal Wholeness. Each symbol is an ever-expanding illuminating guide and transformer, that contains the part and the Whole of the Spiritual Path and the Spiritual Healing you are connecting with. Always use all of them in consecutive togetherness even though one may seem to be a key energy in how you are connecting with Reiki at that time. They support one another and you and together are more powerful than split.

Once initiated into the forms of the symbols in Reiki 11 and Reiki Master levels, you will be shown how to draw the symbols and the sequence of each stroke. Always draw them, rather than just memorising how they look as there is an ever-increasing power connection between you and the meaning of each Reiki Symbol each time you do so. Always repeat their names three times after drawing each symbol. What is named can be claimed!

The sequential way I use Reiki Symbols is:

Choku Rei

I demand the Power of the Universe
(that I may connect with),

Hon Sha Ze Sho Nen,

The Buddha in me sees the Buddha in you
(enabling)

Sei Hei Ki

The key to the understanding the truth of Consciousness itself
and to who I truly am and can be
(through this awareness),

Dai Ko Myo

The Great Light Shines

The most Radiant Light of Truth, of Divinity, of healing, shines
within and outwith
and is available for all sentient beings.

Coda

The Reiki Principles

When I connect with the timelessness of Universal Wholeness, with Reiki, with Truth, I am brought to a moment by moment place of never-ending Now. And so I humbly present an amended offering of the Reiki Principles, which reflect this awareness free from the confines and limitations of linear time.

The Reiki Principles as Originally Taught to Me are:

Just for today, I will not be angry

Just for today, I will not worry

Just for today, I will be grateful

Just for today, I will do my work honestly

Just for today, I will be kind to every living thing

Amended Offering of the Reiki Principles:

I choose Peace

I choose Mindfulness

I choose Gratitude

I choose Self-honesty

I choose Loving-kindness to all Sentient-beings

Epilogue

My Lineage

Medicine Buddha

Dr. Mikao Usui

Dr. Chujiro Hayashi

Hawaya K. Takata

Phyllis Lei Furumoto

Ma Devi Subuddhi, Carell Ann Farmer (1st April 1982)

Ma Deva Pyaso, Eileen Dezouche (27th October 1985)

Ma Rikta, Shanti, Sigrid Rubens (18th October 1989)

Mynavati (23rd July 1995)

This year is the 25th anniversary of my Initiation as a Reiki Master. (2020) In the Bible, this number is considered as Grace upon Grace. But it is also the number of relationship and I cannot imagine a more Divinely perfect time to share in my relationship with you, the reader of this book, any Grace I have received through the Grace of Divine Will and Love.

In my Journey to Reiki and the Journey beyond, I have encountered many great beings who have inspired me and helped me. I have been instructed by them and have been cared for by them. These wonderful, enlightened beings endeavoured to take me beyond my mind. I was turned inside out and moulded anew. But no matter how I grew and how much I learned, I did not outgrow Reiki. At each step Reiki reflected and encompassed my growth. My experience with Reiki changed dramatically as I changed and over the years I realized that Reiki was me. Reiki, was a reflection of who I really am. All I needed to do was be aware of this. That, this connection, is a moving, spiralling, transforming mirror of my ever, eternal, increasing Oneness with everything and everyone and beyond.

I began this book with saying that Reiki is not a tool or a technique. Reiki is not something to learn about and from which to move on from, to grow out of. The initiations, the symbols, the hidden mysteries and depths increasingly reveal themselves as the Reiki Path continues to unfold, revealing an ever-deepening blossoming and understanding of Reiki. Here is a little of my story of unfoldment.

It was the summer of 1993 and in a few weeks I was about to leave for what I believed would be a year-long sabbatical in

India. This was my first encounter with Reiki through a Finnish Reiki Master who arrived at my doorstep in Edinburgh, having travelled from time spent in the Spiritual Community in Findhorn. I was a practicing Spiritual Healer, a member of the National Federation of Spiritual Healers and also practiced a potent emotional energy release healing, but Reiki was all very new to me and I did not know if I wanted to really do it.

But, here was a Reiki Master literally on my doorstep who was available and who wished to also learn from me. We felt a connection with one another and we shared healing methods. I trusted the connection with this sincere Reiki Master and underwent my Reiki1 and Reiki11 Initiations with her.

Within a few months I was living in Sikkim, in the Himalayas with a dear Rinpoche I had met in Edinburgh and his family and I was at times astounded at how, while walking in the Himalayas, I met people who knew about Reiki. I had the grace of practicing Reiki healing relationship connections with Rinpoche and his family.

I discovered how Tibetan Buddhism had its own branch of healing that was very similar to Reiki, using symbols with similar ideas of connection to healing, although I was not so interested at the time in pursuing this.

A few years later, under the direction of Rinpoche, I joined with Papaji, (Sri H.W.L Poonja) who was a well-known Enlightened Advaita Master in Lucknow. I had undergone intense physical and spiritual challenges and spiritual openings while staying in the Himalayas and having visited Bodhgaya on Pilgrimage, it was now approaching winter and was too cold for me as a convalescent with a vulnerable energy system and so the warmer climate in Lucknow, although still cool, was a kinder offering for me.

Papaji inspired, protected, named me and guided me. He was the most beautiful spiritual father and through his blessings, I was later initiated into Reiki Master in Lucknow by one of his devotees. I have continued to use the name he gave me of Mynavati.

In 1996, I met my beloved Guru Sri Sathya Sai Baba and through time and His invitation, remained permanently for many years near to Swami's ashram in Puttaparthi, South India. I stayed up to Swami's physical death on 24th April 2011 and for a few years afterwards. Swami's teachings on Advaita the teachings of non-duality that I was introduced to by Papaji and His kindness and compassion, deepened my understanding of

Absolute Reality and its relationship with Reiki and inspired me towards an eagerness for service and deeper healing.

I have expanded and grown but I have grown and expanded into Reiki rather than out of Reiki. I have expanded and grown into the energy of God. For me Reiki is as limitless and as endless as the energy of God and the Loving Force of God. But then, it should be as it's the same isn't it? Reiki is Universal Wholeness. Universal Wholeness is Love, Love is God.

I now feel blessed to live in The Highlands in Scotland although a part of my heart remains and will always remain in sacred India and in particular in Puttaparthi, the abode of Swami.

I do not give a biography in this book of Dr. Mikao Usui, Dr. Chujiro Hayashi or Hawaya K Takata although I feel deeply grateful to them all and I leave this to your own research. There are various accounts of Usui's life and how Reiki started, some universally accepted and some conflicting and I am not going to delve into this aspect because for me it is pointless.

I know Reiki through the empowerments and Initiations I have been given. I know Usui though the transmissions I have been blessed to receive, I know all I need to know of those who came after him through these energies. I am grateful for them all for being the instruments of a spiritual healing force that has changed the world of healing and the lives and healing of countless people. I am grateful for their commitment and good intentions. I am grateful for everyone who tries to be true to who they are and what they believe and who exhibits compassion and loving-kindness in their daily work and lives.

I am grateful to you, the reader, for reading this book and for sharing your sacred time.

Thank you

Loving blessings
Mynavati

June 2020

Books written by the Author

Bardo of Becoming - A unique novel of the Journey in the 'In-between' by Mynavati. Fully Revised Second Edition available on Amazon Kindle.

Be Happy with Prayer, Meditation and Affirmation by Mynavati.
Fully Revised Second Edition available on Amazon Kindle.

Chakra Power - How to Heal the Emotions by Mynavati.
Fully Revised Third Edition available on Amazon Kindle.

Divine Play by Mynavati, digitally available on
www.mynavati.com

Forty-nine Days by Mynavati, Fully Revised Second Edition available on Amazon Kindle and in Paperback 2023.

Heal by Mynavati.
Fully Revised Second Edition available on Amazon Kindle.

Meditations by Mynavati

Over 40 healing healing and insight meditations by Mynavati are available on youtube at:

www.youtube.com/c/meditationsbymynavati

Mynavati freely offers daily Distant Healing to all from her website **www.mynavati.com**

She conducts Reiki Retreats in The Scottish Highlands for the Initiation of sincere seekers in the Reiki Attunements on all levels. If you wish to contact Mynavati to know more about Reiki and the Reiki retreats please email Mynavati at mynavati@mynavati.com

Reflections,
(including writings on Vasanas and Habitual Patterning)
Inspirational Thoughts for the Day, freely given distant healing and more at **www.mynavati.com**

Books on Reiki

There are as many Reiki Books as there are ideas about Reiki. Please read what you are drawn to and those you feel connected with. I suggest that you read books that have researched into and explored as much as possible the true history of Mikao Usui and Reiki as this book does not cover this aspect.

Practical books that contain Reiki hand-placements will be helpful for those who wish to seek Reiki Initiation and practice Reiki hands-on healing as, again, this book does not cover hand-placements.

Books on Medicine Buddha and Relevant Buddhism

A Guide to the Bodhisattva's Way of Life Paperback – 1 Dec. 1992 by Shantideva (Author)

Medicine Buddha Teachings by Khenchen Thrangu, Tashi Nangyal (Editor), Yeshe Gyamtso (Translator) Snow Lion, April 07, 2004

Sadhana of the Medicine Buddha: A Short Root Text by Dudjom Rinpoche
Published by Yeshe Melong (first published 1998) **ISBN** 096213712X

The Wish-Fulfilling Jewel; The Practice of Guru Yoga According to the Longchen
Nyingthig Tradition, Shambhala, Boston and London, 1987

Books by Papaji

Truth is Paperback by H. W. L Poonja (Author) – 1 Mar. 2000

Wake Up and Roar: Satsang with H W L Poonja, Vol. II, Pacific Center Publishing, 1993.

Books by or about Sri Sathya Sai Baba

Sathyam Sivan Sudaram Series (Life Story of Bhagawan Sri Sathya Sai Baba), by Professor Kasturi, Sri Sathya Sai Books & Publications Trust, Prashanti Nilayam, A.P. 515134, India

Upanishad Vahini by Bhagavan Sri Sathya Sai Baba, Sri Sathya Sai Books & Publications Trust, Prasanthi Nilayam, A.P., India. 1999.

Sathya Sai Speaks Series, Discourses by Bhagavan Sri Sathya Sai Baba, Vol. I-XXX, Sri Sathya Sai Books & Publications Trust, Prasanthi Nilayam, A.P. 515134, India.

Vedic Books

The Ashtavakra Gita, translated by Hari Prasad Shastri, Shanti Sadan, 1992.

The Ramayana

The Supreme Yoga by Yoga Vashistha

The Upanishads

The Vedas

Printed in Great Britain
by Amazon

19460228R00067